Dear Sal

poems by
Jeremy Radin

not a cult.

los angeles, ca
notacult.media

Printed in the USA

Radin, Jeremy

1st edition.

ISBN: 978-1-945649-03-5

Edited by Elaina Ellis
Cover design by Cassidy Trier
Editorial design by Ian DeLucca

not a cult.
Los Angeles, CA

Printed in the United States of America

For Art Cohan and Samantha Sloyan.
This is a waltz, remember?

Contents

"Every heart / to love will come / but like a refugee."
—*Leonard Cohen*

Dear Sal,

In a room on the river
we breathed deep the honeysuckle,
kissed against a suspended boat,
waltzed to a brass band playing
in a distant park. You fed me dark
bread slathered in butter
as is I were one of the soldiers
in your ward & I did not speak of
the French, the Germans, my mouth
too full of sweetnesses. Your hands
aglow, you touched me
with such unbearable attention.
Accurate fingers unlaced
the slaughter. Numbers
& the names of countries
crumbled in your eyes.

She lays her hand in the mud and leaves it.

A firefly crawls across her shoulder.

Dogs moan on the horizon line.

The stars sleep standing up.

She puts a piece of the river in her pocket.

Whatever Time There Is in a Life Is a Lifetime

All day long I see people
      kiss—in movie theaters,

on the bus, in between the beads
      of rain. Lovers like

glaciers crashing into each other
      with such a ferocious

tenderness. I hold out
      my hands & they waltz

in my palms. My hands
      a boathouse, the night

a river. I drift through
      streets with eyes closed, grasping

at stars. I wish to catch one, take it
      in my hands & press

my lips to its boiling
      sex. How I wonder what you are

doing now as I watch two people
      leaning in—could be

the first time—under an awning across
      the road. Gottenyu,

this moment—just before, when kiss
      is mere possibility, a hovering,

a bridge being built from
        the center outward, when

it could go either way—to come
        ashore or hurry back

into the ocean. The heart
        a tower of skittish smoke

& somewhere, a soft wind
        rising.

Fabulous Phantoms, I Welcome You!

This I roar each night into the storm.
I open the windows & open the lungs.

> *Fabulous phantoms, I welcome you!*

I strip off my clothes in the whirling frost-
light, beam like the ass of a fat firefly.

> *Fabulous phantoms, I welcome you!*

I cannot imagine anything worse than being
mistaken for a political person.

Each Night the Lithuanian & I Go for a Walk in the Park

When we arrive at the war memorial, she stops
& spits on the tip of her cane, which I place
with a fond ferocity onto the eyeball
of the marble general.

      Each night we feed the bread to the water.

Each night we pour the wine on the stones.

          Each night in this country in this wisecrack

of a world where we are not

              the ones who died.

Dear Sal,

We set a table for the eating of ghosts.

Plates in the shape of history's figure.
Knives in the shape of a nation's border.
Cups in the shape of a dead child's mouth.

   The sky is your mother & fathers' arms

I should mention that we are on a small boat.
I should mention the sea is not made of water.
That continents eat each other in our dreams.

   The sun is the song of your strangled sister

Swallowing ghosts in a room of salt
the aunt the uncle their children & me
the Jew the Jew the Jews & the Jew

the Promised Land looming before us.

Mt. Casanova Tells a Story

Many years ago there was a bakery—a very curious bakery. The man who owned the bakery, he made the finest rugalach in Russia. The bakery was situated under the earth, beneath the original bakery, which had been his parents', and which had been, along with his parents, burned to a crisp in a pogrom. Day in and day out he worked in this bakery—say his parents were somehow wealthy, had been saving to come to America for years. Say he wanted for nothing. Say his ingredients came from where his ingredients came from—the point is he baked rugalach all day long in this little bakery under the earth. As I said, the finest rugalach in all of Russia. But. He sold none of it, gave none of it away, ate none of it himself. Day in and day out he broke the eggs, sifted the flour, rolled the dough, sweating, cursing, singing to himself the songs that bakers sing. And then the trays of steaming rugalach would be placed on the counter to cool until the end of the day when he would feed them to the fire. On and on and no one was ever the wiser. No one knew from this rugalach prodigy (the Rachmaninoff of Rugalach, they would have called him) and because the bakery was under the earth, no one smelled the intoxicating smells. Every night he would trudge home again and go to sleep in his little room, crushed into his little bed by this routine put in place by no one. Living in a constant state of vexation. Trudging home, wracked with vexation, trudging to the bakery, wracked with vexation. Trudging and trudging, to and from—past the butcher, the schoolmaster, the beggar starving to death in the road.

The Citizens of the Delicatessen

"Abacus"
This is the name for me. Out of fashion, a curiosity.
Obsolete number cruncher, coated in dust.

"Kishka Phil"
Has he ever ordered anything else?

"Pants"
They come at least to his armpits. He looks like a man
being swallowed by a corduroy whale.

"The Queen of the Weimaraners"
She has had eight of them, all named "Pierre".

"Have You Heard The One About"
*An endlessness of riddles & jokes. Have you heard the one
about the drunken pigeon? The one about the Martian & the
Jew? The one about Lincoln in the field of spoons? The genie in
the apple? The chemist, the fool, & the invention of America?*

"The Tallow Man"
Forty years in the manufacture of soap, the filthiest person
you will ever meet.

"Mt. Casanova"
At least three hundred & fifty pounds, he claims to be
with a different woman each night. We called him a liar
until he showed us "The Portfolio".

"Little Shofar"
Within the realm of his understanding you will nowhere
find the modulation of volume.

"Shia Bubik"
The Jester-King of Gritsev. Stealer of the White Horse.
Halter of the Pack of Tanks. Lover of Serious Women & a
Real Gutte Neshome.

"The Lithuanian"
She comes in the late hours, apart from the others,
carrying a snow cloud on her back.

"Grandfather Clock"
He sits alone at the corner table. Every hour on the hour
he raises his hand. Three times he speaks a woman's
name, closes his eyes, & is silent.

"The Cantor"
When she sings, somewhere, a mountain.

Dear Sal,

The citizens of the delicatessen
speak of playing chess against
the angels, of singed vests & feathers
piled beside the bed. They raise

wooden canes toward fluorescents,
pronounce a dark & humid question
for which I have no answer. I laugh,
say the river

remembers better than I. My beard,
still, belying nothing. I do not speak
your goyische name, the infinite
space it makes in my mouth.

In winter's belly I wander through
the streets, costumed in the clothing
of a bridegroom. I tighten my tie past
the borders of mercy, burst apart

into the snow.

Bundles of poems in the boathouse rafters.

A pair of owls back-to-back on a fencepost.

She smells the fingerprints left on the dress.

Her mother calls her name twelve times.

Certain songs can be drawn from memory.

Dear Sal,

What a curious relationship has been cultivated
with the animal of my solitude. In the early dark
I watch it sniff around the room—little nebula,
winged hedgehog, glittering in the almost-light.
I feed it from my palms & I feed it my palms.
Piece by piece I tender my urgency. Returning
from the office I find it hovering in the center
of the apartment. I sleep curled around it, blurry
chandelier. At the delicatessen I pay the girl who
smiles at me & there it is, waiting in my wallet.
It gnaws at my fingers & I excuse myself swiftly.
I am, even after all these years, an utter virtuoso
of compliance. *You chose me*, it reminds, sighing
at my paltry desire. When I came home from
the fields of your vehement care it ordered me
to kneel. I ground my knees into the carpet.
It spread
       & spread
             its wings

Now the River Tells What it Saw

Red smoke. Oysters in the trash. Pearls ground in a machine.
Hatchets hung from a windmill. The weaponization of a
sycamore. This country. And then the wonder. The softness of a
great distance from war. The very opposite of the world. The
man becomes the woman becomes the man becomesthe evening
in question—a festival of hungry & silent wings.

Now the Owls

o yes   that   how remarkable   what you do   with each other
*   your terrible   bodies   becoming*
*   suddenly incapable   of what   they continue*
to do   to our bodies   to the one   body   o g-d
*   when they   made   the sound*
*   of their true   body   we could not*
help   ourselves   the nation of us
*   rushing   toward   those countless*
twinkling mice   knowing   this time
*   we would take them   in our claws*

Now the Stars

Do You Think You Can Understand This

                                  A Birth

We Moved Toward Each Other

We Made Ready

We Made Ready   *For The Welcome*

The Tallow Man

(digging in his dirty, dirty ear):

Here's the thing—
each day I wake up,
fry a couple eggs,

and make up
new songs
about the frying
of eggs.

Some days
I take myself
to the movies—

love that Bogart—
he sure knows how
to hold a gun.

Some days, I go
down and look
at the fish.

The orange ones
are terrific
and then there are
the blue ones.

Some days, I feed
the strays—Checkers,
Houdini, St. Augustine.

What do the angels
know about
contentment?

I've learned
when the baker
pulls bread
from the oven.

I've learned
where the swans
will gather.

The teeth-
marks have
fallen out
of my heart.

Some animals
warn us with
startling colors.

I smell the way
I have to smell.

Dear Sal,

Plopped on the bus stop bench, my father's phantom & I are the consummate expression of a rich & inherited solitude. I stare ahead, cross-legged, fists in pockets. He pretends at the perusing of a paper. The Plymouth has given out again, this time with a foul sputter like blood bubbling in the neck of a goat. Revelers flow in & out of a bar across the road—the sort where men go to feel as if they're hunting on a close friend's private island. In & out they swagger, sabers of Cossacks, analyzing strategy, plunging, glinting, back into the pursuit. The quarry? Women so existent I feel like a vacuum. They smoke thin cigarettes in shimmering clusters, the smoke doing imitations of their necks. Do not ask if they are beautiful. These are the women you look away from quickly & try to focus on where you excel. For me, the dignity of numbers, the absurdities of horror. My father's phantom asks what I think they talk about. I shrug my shoulders, remain silent. I do not know how to look at anyone but through the lens of my undesirability. A woman runs across the street with hair like a collapsing fire. Her body is a country. My body is a small blemish on the bottom of the ocean. My father's phantom says, *Tell me, boychik, tell me about this woman you love.* What can I tell him? The fog hovers around a street-lamp. *Look papa,* I say to the absence, *you can see the hem of her gown.*

Ghazal for a Truly Magnificent Dress

Burning beds in a field I command the light, unleash it in
        the direction of your dress.
I repeat your name to a cavalry of stars, hold to their
        noses a section of your dress.

You find me trembling like a goat at the altar—starving,
        skinny, my hair a ghost's nest.
You take me inside to bind my wound in water, nourish
        me on the confection of your dress.

A basket of peaches underneath your arm, delight like an
        orchard budding in your chest,
you stroll through the seething honeysuckle, its scent the
        only explanation for your dress.

A sycamore sags on the side of a road—bones of a
        forgotten saint, unsung & under-blessed.
May we be delivered up from her roots, may we bloom in
        the fertile salvation of her dress.

How dark is the sum of the unburied dead? They scale the
        moonlight & bellow distress.
What relief awaits when you unfold the fabrics & open
        the organization of your dress.

Refugees cascade from the mouths of whales. In a
  language of no they are the sole surviving *yes.*
I came from the dark with a war in my teeth, seeking
  clemency here in the nation of your dress.

I die in in the tub as the coffee boils — I am lifted by the
  angels, I am lifted by regrets.
I am brought back to life in a room on the river, howling
  against the negation of your dress.

Dear Sal,

In a darkened kitchen you cook supper
for a family that will not speak your name.
Steam unfurls from the stewpot, assumes
the shape of a debutante gown. Your pa
stomps a hunt's mud off his boots, gloves
slick with deers' dreams—he is growling
at the dark again, spitting through the dull
black hills of his teeth. Your brother screws
his wife on a rug of shotgun shells. Your ma
bathes in a slaughtered piano, sings a war
against music, anthem of your expulsion.

What would we do without our families?

Mine, sentries of earth, exchanging
voices in my memory. Let us pay them
a visit, eat soup thick with burial hymns
& moonlight. My papa, of course, will
begin a big speech & my sister will make
a joke beneath her breath. Mama will
sing some blistering prayer that calls
your other brother to us—your darling
brother, eaten by his government—yes,
he will be there as well, beaming in his
uniform, bullets falling out of his heart,
blooming before they hit the ground.

Dear Sal,

My response to the news has become visceral,
as though the fighting occurs between my guts.

This war & that, over & over. Numbers themselves
are not grim, just what we learn to attribute them to.

Another round for the dead, another round of dead.
I would thrust a saber through the belly of heaven

if it meant they would return to kiss their mothers'
ruined cheeks, their children's bewilderment away.

Grandfather Clock sits moaning at his table, the Queen
of the Weimaraners wishes to console him, but look,

she clutches a half-burnt photograph. & the Lithuanian
has no more room in her mouth—all the black flowers.

I don't know how to tell you about your brother. How
he dances with my sister in a ballroom of clouds—you

wonder how I know this but I've always known. My curse,
to feel in the winds the manufacture of ghosts, it is not

something I can help. Snow falls onto the courtyard &
I catch it in my palm, put it to my ear the way a child

would a seashell. *Murder in the hundred-thousands,*
I saw it while falling on this field or that, they were

carted away like sacks of flour. Presumably, I think,
to salvage the bullets. What isn't a business? Slicing

onions for an omelet I open my palm & foam
at the wound with gold.

Tell Me About the Mosquitoes, Sal

My blood is a song in my mother's mouth.
My blood is the hem of my sister's dress.
My blood is my father's silent surrender.

Tell me about the mosquitoes, Sal.

My blood is a ghost-wave radio.
My blood is a city of refugee children.
My blood is soap for a Frenchman's hands.

Tell me about the mosquitoes, Sal.

My blood is a book I can't read my way out of.
My blood is a mirror I can't see.

Tell me about the mosquitoes, Sal.

Tell them about me.

The bottle full of little gasps.

A synagogue built from cigarette butts.

Bells rusting in the honeysuckle.

Winter wraps its tail around her neck.

Two spirits haunt the same house but never meet.

Dear Sal,

Desire is a Plymouth idling on my chest.
A woman sings on the radio
& I punch the Lord all over the place. What
are these hands even for? Dry nights I drag
them across my belly & listen to the sound —
a distant snow saying your name over & over.
What did the Tallow Man say about the eggs?
We will never be any use again…
In the office I daydream your crackling laugh
& magpies & kestrels & cormorants surge
from the bottoms of my pant legs & we both
know that this is not what happens. I touch

this part of myself so rarely. When I do, what
savagery blooms within my dreams. Once I beat
a man to death with a torah. In another, with
a smoked salmon. & once, with a burning cedar
tree. I dreamt I murdered a man with a burning
cedar tree. We were standing in a vaulted room
that was at once a subway station & synagogue
& there was a man playing a violin & there was
a burning cedar tree & I tore it from the ground
& beat the man to death with it. Do you understand
what I am saying to you? Please, Sal, please —
you must never kiss me again.

Little Shofar Offers an Opinion

*THERE'S A LOTTA DIFFERENT WAYS YOU
CAN THINK ABOUT THE WORD COWARD FOR
INSTANCE THERE'S THE USUAL WAY YOU
KNOW SHAME SHAME SHAME BUT THAT ISN'T
SO INTERESTING TO ME IF YOU ASK ME I THINK
THE BIG OBVIOUS PROBLEM THERE IS FIRST
THEY JUMP ONTO THE TABLES AND SHOUT
AND NEXT THING EVERYONE'S WEARING THE
SAME BOOTS YOU WANNA BE THERE OR NOT
IF WE'RE GONNA TALK ABOUT COWARD
FIRST WE GOTTA TALK ABOUT TERROR
TERROR'S WHY WE'RE HERE IT'S WHY WE'RE
HAVING THIS CONVERSATION I MEAN WHAT
GOOD IS A DEAD HERO WE GOTTA CHANGE
THE WHOLE ATTITUDE IF WE'RE EVER
GONNA LOVE EACH OTHER THAT'S JUST
BASIC ARITHMETIC I'M SAYING HOW CAN
YOU MAKE LOVE TO A NUMBER HOW CAN
YOU HOLD A HOLE IN THE AIR HERE'S WHAT
I THINK COWARD THIS COWARD THAT I'M
TELLING YOU BE A MAN IS THE END OF US ALL
I MEAN SURE PAL IF YOU WANNA TAKE THE
BULLET YOU GO RIGHT AHEAD I'LL BE HERE
WITH MY SANDWICH AND COFFEE SWAPPING
STORIES WITH THE OTHER COWARDS AWAY
FROM THE TRAINS AND THE GUNS AND THE
WOMEN WITH KNIVES HIDDEN IN THEIR HAIR*

I Will Tell This in the Only Way I Can Tell It

The grove in which we grew the bells.

Sneaking in with the other children.

Shooing the cuckoos out of the trees.

Year after year after year after year.

Through the gate with Mama & Papa.

Harvesting sound for the silent winter.

Eventually we shouldered the ladders.

Strapping baskets of music to mules.

Houses in blizzards fat with ringing.

The origin stories of sorrow & stars.

& war after war after war after war.

Arriving again with guns & thunder.

Bells crumpling under the numbers.

The punctual arrival of bullets.

Bell after bell after bell after child

& now we will speak of the weather.

Dear Sal,

The name of these purple flowers? I'm dying
to know. I can say only that they are purple

& the shape of me not knowing what to do
with my hands in your absence. What name

for this shape? Explain as well how you sang me
to sleep & the song was a song my mother

composed, years after her death. I can see you
moving through the hospital wing, administering

to the blood-shock boys in their new masks
of distance. Such a gutte neshome you are, pulling

yourself together in the janitor's closet. In other
news, a pigeon has come to the window. In other

news it is windy, & I am very frightened.

The Queen of the Weimaraners Introduces the Urns

*I know, I know, I know what the Law says. I don't care. I need
them with me. Pierre, Pierre, Pierre, Pierre, Pierre, Pierre,
Pierre, my friends, my wraiths, my ghoulish anthem against
abandonment. My girlhood was eaten by alarms. The dry slap
of the boot-sole. God sat drooling in her underwear. Chicago,
Alphabet City, San Francisco. The blue czar hulking on the
threshold. Each friend, a bank of memory. Here, the blazing
daisy. Here, the wooden spoon breaching the bound of the hem.
The vanished husband. The milkman dead in the doorway.*

*Companionship should not be spoken of. Let it be the noble
mystery. My husband used to say—something—but I was
caught in the storm of the eye. Gray, gray, gray. My loves. My
beloveds. My Basherts.* (Here she takes down an urn) *A
fortune teller told me we that met in Barcelona. The 1700s. I
was weeping by the sea. Winter scraped its knuckles down my
back. Something had been lost—then a voice
behind me. Pierre. We married in the fall. We died. We found
each other again. Already we are ghosts. Child, what will be
        has been*

*and ceased to be. And we will go on moaning at the window,
waiting for our master to return.*

Dear Sal,

There was a treaty signed. There were witnesses: a moth, an opened ledger.

On one side of the table, I sat. On the other side, my longing. I was dressed in a blue three-piece suit. He was in the nude, humming a brutal earworm of a tune.

There was no paper. We signed the wind & my silence began to glow, a candle beckoning within a cellar. The blaze of my sex, bound by law.

Surely the moth brought the news to the others. Even those in the rafters of the boathouse the night we were so flagrant with our tenderness.

When one builds a god & then kills the god, a mausoleum is constructed — you bury yourself or there are the penances.

A year ago the numbers began to tremble. They whispered disgust & switched costumes in the dark. Vines curled from the mouth of the shofar, turned to tendrils of stone.

That night I flayed off my own skin, stitched it back into a tent in which I await the black sound of the horn.

I tiptoe even through my dreams. I will not return. We must carve the moment from our minds & give it back to the river.

Sal, the moths are at the window.

An agreement is an agreement.

Dear Sal,

Bad news first: the pigeons
have not yet made me their king
even thought I speak the language
& adhere to every custom. Also,
the bread I tried to bake? Full,
again, of roses. Packed tight
inside like fugitives from God
knows where. & for the twelfth
night in a row I dreamt of snakes
with spiders' legs. I wake
& the bedsheets are on the floor
across the room, the pillow spins
in the ceiling fan's arms. & too,
I heard the knives in the kitchen
whispering my Hebrew name.
It sounded like opening an old
book drenched in blood. If I
were to answer…well Sal,
now we've arrived at
the good news.

Kishka Phil, Through a Mouthful of Kishka

One of these days

> *whether the Lord*

> *is willing*

> *or not*

> *we will all*

> *get*

> *some sleep*

Dear Sal,

Tonight I am an ox.

Hauling a cart loaded with something
alive or dying
across the frost-blistered steppe of my apartment.

The night tallies the loyal
by the lights left on in the windows.

Bright & separate as yolks.

You are waltzing with a well-
dressed man in a church
basement lit by little candles.

I trudge as if through snow,
whispering a broken vow,
this gray plea for exoneration.

The thing in the cart is growing now
into a death or terrible new life.

A darkness dragged
through a darker darkness.

Heavy
as a forgotten language.

Possible
as a weapon.

Eggs! Eggs! Eggs! Eggs!

& so I learn to pass desire
     like a kidney stone. I lay
        in bed, grinding
            my teeth into snow,
       tearing at my knuckles
   & sweating. A star

steamrolls through
     my body, brash magnet, gathering
        the angels of silence,
           boiling them into song. Mama said

        our children await
     their arrival in a corner of space, climb
quasars & build dolls
     out of luminous dust. I adore
        my children too much to let them
           wind up here. So I bear

        the pain, bear the pain. Crawl
     into the fog like a prayer & vanish.
Replace my flesh with text.

     As much as I long to see again
        how you arrange
           your sorrow in the woods,

     Bashert, there is no choice.

Refasten my robe at the waist.
Mend the dirt. Close the door.

I will not inter you
in my history. Love,

I spare you the love.

She reads the same word over and over.

A vulture circles its own reflection.

A mausoleum full of unfinished letters.

Her footfalls at midnight in the pattern of a waltz.

A faucet runs until the pre-dawn.

More About the Pigeons

I know very little.
Of this, they constantly
      remind me. *You*

they say   *know*
        very little.

It's just that when my father's
body was hauled
from that room, they were all

      I noticed. Strange

that it is night, I thought, &
the sky
is full   of pigeons.

I heard them   shudder,

     saw the specks of light
between the gaps

        in their feathers.

Pigeons of the world
     by day dispersing,
making dirty circles
over cops & opera singers,

       at evening
gather in the sky

to make, again,
the dark.   Last night

I dreamt
     you slipped

    from a shadow
as the earth slips
    from her gown
       of pigeons

& I could not
    get off the floor
for the weight
       of all
    that I do not know.

Standing at the Station with Grandfather Clock

Who was she, I ask. The old man turns, takes
my wrist. His beard becomes a snow, whirling

away from his face, assuming the shape of a house.
Two candled windows rumble towards us. The city
is gone. In its place, a shtetl. I can no longer tell

the difference between snow & stars. His papery skin
flakes away, becomes the storm, the house, wagoned
road, distant pine. Nearer, nearer, the candles blaze.

The house smells of beet soup & bread. A woman's voice
haloes the roof. Next to me, a young man—
shaggy hair spilling from his cap, circular spectacles,
beard

the color of hills at night. A brightness tumbles out
of his eyes, a bundle of small white flowers.
The night goes wild with silence. & then, of course,

the hooves.

Dear Sal,

A goat heart has appeared
in the basket of apricots.

The answer is yes to your next
question & the sound is colossal,
the size of an arena.

The walls of my apartment shake
with goat operas & I
do not even mind

that the apricots are ruined
& the banks have foreclosed
on my unhappiness

& time is a goat heart

we spend our entire lives
chewing to the other side of.

Beyond this wall of pulsing redness
there is a grove of cedar trees—women
falling into the earth, green gowns
flying up over their heads.

Apricots grow from the cedar trees,
but goat hearts instead of apricots.

An old woman eats
from a basket of goat hearts
& is shocked to find one apricot

& to answer your question,
no, & the stillness overwhelms.

This woman is called mother,
or so my blood tells me. Have I
spoken yet of her to you?

Instead I will speak
of a goat heart in a basket
of apricots, please. Instead
of saying her name

I will bite into a living machine
with a prayer inside it
& she who had my eyelashes
& waits within a cedar grove
will bite into a perfect stillness

& someplace else a goat will fall
& an apricot grove will catch on fire

& you will reach into a basket
of nothing & pull out a fucking star.

A Joke from Have You Heard the One About

Have you heard the one about the man
who stands near the edge of a great sea
somewhere in the forests of Germany?

He stands and stands, how long he stands!
A deer approaches and chews off his clothes
and still the man stands. A vulture constructs

a nest in his hair and still he stands
as though it were an edict. A lizard slithers
up the man's legs, all the way up to

the vulture's nest, steals one of the vulture's
eggs and still, the man, he does not stir.
And bees build a hive between his legs.

And a bear does what a bear does. But does
the man move, even an inch? No, he does
not move, even an inch. Years

go by! In autumn the man is mantled
in leaves, in winter the man is mantled
in snow, in spring the flowers clamber

up his elbows, in summer the sun peels
back his hair. He is waiting for the water
to return. The sea, you see, is empty—

and though it rains the way in Germany
it rains, the sea does not become filled.
And though it snows the way in Germany

it snows, and the snow melts as snow melts, still,
the sea, it will not fill. There it sits — a grand
emptiness, a sublime emptiness,

and the man stands — a grand emptiness, a sublime
emptiness. They consider each other, this pair
of emptinesses. And after a hundred, a thousand

years, one of them opens their mouth to speak.
That is the way the joke begins. The punchline
is you, waiting for the punchline.

Villanelle for the Citizens, Ending in an Address to You

Of war & good smoked fish
we speak, Citizens of the Deli
who move our hands too much.

We open our mouths & pigeons
struggle forth, coarse historians
of war & good smoked fish.

At home I wrap the past in sheets of
absurdity. How many has it taken—
we, who move our hands too much?

Rain falls from umbrellas like friends
from memory. After funerals, we dream
of war & good smoked fish.

Stitch a coat of numbers. Protected
by math, we question the wind: *why us,
we, who move our hands too much?*

A graying sun flutters in my chest
like a shot duck, dies in a lake
of war & good smoked fish.

Around another coffin we gather,
sing again, welcome old ghosts
who move our hands—too much

time away, you smoke on a whisper
of river. Sal, I am so goddamned tired
of war.
                    Our hands, too much.

Dear Sal,

I should tell you
I am a clumsy man.

Yolk stains
each extremity.

I speak in storms
of hammers, tear grace
off its hinges.

In the dark desire
escapes me
& bruises the air.

We are breathing in our rooms
yet still I grieve, still

the Kaddish falls
from this sack of compliance
I've packed my worship into.

The figures your mouth
made upon my skin
are rumbling tonight.

I try to write
their names
but fail.

I am a longing
locked in the body of failure,
attempting to arrange the failure

back into the shape
of your hands.

Shia Bubik Delivers a History

You know from where I came, all the old classics: how I soiled
myself in a cherry tree, helped a farmer with his calf and it
*   pished all down my back.*

Gritsev. A nothing place. Running with my brother, the
daredevil. We stole some farmer's white horse, galloped through
*   town to dazzle a girl. My brother*

the maniac. He lives now in Paterson — imagine, he lives! He
laughs at things the body does. A moron and I miss him but I
*   hated Jersey. In Gritsev —*

a bobkes place, big as a flea on a donkey's toches — a girl lived
who was named for a flower. Existing unbeknownst to us. In
*   Gritsev! Population: the freckles*

on this girl's face. She read storybooks, apparently, where the
bodies now are buried, traded with the rabbi's son. Tended
*   chickens. Helped her*

father with the cows. This and that. And one day at a theater in
Paterson they meet. Imagine! My brother is not a religious man.
*   But every morning*

his wife rises to her knees. He says, such an idiot, when she
lights the Sabbath candles, when she beckons the flames into
*   her eyes, they obey, they spring*

from the wicks and into her face, light her up like a lantern,
and she takes a mouthful of wine, holds it in her cheeks, and
*   their little house glows a deep,*

deep red. And they waltz at the bus stop to a tune that he hums.
And they swing on the children's swing in the park. A miracle
in this world, for a fool

to receive a fool. They make love as if love were made for them,
as if God called them up a mountain and bestowed them the
tablets of honey. Look at us,

Abacus. We are becoming old. Is it enough for us, to sit with our
blintzes & tell the same stories over and over? Is it enough to
die on our own accord?

Gritsev. Paterson. Can't you see what a marvel this is? You are
hunted by gentle, by holy things, and you don't stand a chance.

Dear Sal,

After all these years, today, I reach my age. To celebrate
I eat egg salad on rye the size of a Buick. There is the
mishegas & there is the mishegas. The man who gave me
a voice, he did not even speak the language, but still—do
you know what the word Bashert means? I would reenter
the thieving jaws of Europe for you, eat mayonnaise on
the Eiffel Tower, sing to the Rhine in the language of my
people. If that, Bashert, is your wish. What have I been
trying to say about desire? Stuffing egg salad into my
mouth. It's not something I can afford. *But what good is an
egg?* At this time of day the park is almost empty. Bashert,
imagine! Just the two of us, strolling hand in hand, the
beast of longing whimpering under our shoes. We call it
longing because it takes forever. I am ( ) years old. How
can it matter? I hope at least I made you laugh. What do
you call the most Jewish fish? The *anchoyvey.* Came up
with that as the moon ate my hands. Ah yes, the shadow is
mine. My beard, thick with mustard & seeds. What do you
call a garden on the bottom of a river? When the garden
rises up in you, Bashert, what do you call?

Dear Sal,

For nearly a year I have been building a word.
Hammering letters together, welding with a torch
that shoots an eggshell-colored flame. I began

my work while recalling the unthinkable details
of you: in your scrubs, a column of attention,
whispering restorative lies to the lost. The way

when gesturing your pinky unlocks the ark of the air,
Gottenyu, your pinky! How she stands apart
from all the others. They, a cluster of gossips—she,

preening, disturbing the sensibilities. It is almost
finished, the word. I would say it here but I wish
to say it in your house. To your father, mother,

brother & his twelve-gauge altar. Instead I holler
recipes at lizards, cry Kaddish over birds that dash
their brains out on the door. The word is staging

a coup in my mouth. Sing to me, Bashert, once
more. There is not enough room in the world
for your silence.

I Tell Pants About You & He Says

Oh goodness, what a thing, what a thing! I'm thankful we are
sitting down!
     My knees, they've turned to little fogs!
My heart makes the sounds of a night in the swamp! Stars
unzipping their dresses!
     Toads and their heroic belching! Oh, Friend, I want to
know everything!
Don't tell me more!
     I can't decide!

I want to parade you down Market Street on my shoulders!
     What color is her hair—no, no, don't say!
I'll imagine a rope of starlight falling over a freckled shoulder!
     I could kiss you! Kissing!
I see it in your future!
     Look, here in my cup of coffee!
Of course, the wedding will have to be spectacular!

     Processions of geese, clarinets and cellos!
Baskets and baskets of hyacinth petals! What a blessing, what
a blessing!
     Oh, I hope I'm not getting ahead of myself.
But it is exactly that I must hope!

     God bless all we've kept safe from our love.
God bless the bottles and God bless the dust.
     The absence brushing our bodies through its hair.

But o you bleary
and brimming thing!
        O you bumbling
bumbling marvel!

What is all of this but proof
        that all of this
                is working?

Barring touch, the river is demolished.

Barring touch, the revolution fails.

Barring touch, the body is a dream of water.

We make a god of distance.

We are occupied by silence.

Amazing the Things You Get So Used to That You Don't Know Them Anymore

Bashert, we have been buried alive
in all that will make us
invincible

Longing, an empire
falling from the ceiling

The Lithuanian Speaks

*No no no is no good. For so long alone? Is breaking! A person
no is clock, only for see the pass of time. Hands we need hands
hands! To make HaShem singing here. Inside. From kestrels to
seagulls to vulgar pigeons you come, and space only your body
to hold against? My friend. Is no good! Inside. Inside swans
still. Yes, you no say is not! Swans and the memory of your
darlingsong. Am I saying right? Your darlingsong, your, ech!
You to touch must fly. Is true! You to touch, yes.
Goodbye the dust   and go.*

Dear Sal,

An ancient city of light is buried
in my chest. Before the French (or was it
the Germans) my father tucked it in there
& placed me on a boat. *Be a good little
smuggler & forget our names.* At night
I opened my mouth to the water & strange
shapes came to investigate. I begged them
to absolve me. *The Lord spared the animals
guilt, for in the wild everything that lives
lives instead of something else.* A quiet life
has turned me earth—soft mud & eggshell.
When you kissed me a stove flicked on,
generators began to hum. We left each
other like altars in a bombing run. In this
room where you are not, night lowers itself
all around me. I stare at my fingers—little
archaeologists clutching brilliant shovels.
They leap from my hands & begin to dig.
After unsayable years, the clay, remnants
of lamps, & then the city, & then the light.
The archaeologists cart its body to a fountain
where old women drop their buckets & fall,
wailing like chimneys, to their knees. A boy
is healed when his wound is brought & bared
before the glow. Of course the government
intervenes, as always they must intervene,
orders it cloaked in metal & dropped upon
a country—but there it wraps the children
in shawls of unfused atoms, their mothers
in gowns of light-silk, & fathers fall asleep
in trenches as their rifles morph into violins
that play as we waltz in a room on the river,
our shadows melting into one shadow, &

Sal, I thought—we thought we were
dead—but we are not yet
finished dying.

Dear Sal,

As far as the Name goes
I have known the Name
in sugar-dusted blintzes
& books of numbers.

Never in the brutal
choices of men
that end in names
becoming numbers.

As far as names go
I've been unsuccessful
in cursing a single one.

All my wrath
embezzled
by longing.

As far as longing goes
I dragged my ghost
across the ocean
searching for signs
of the opposite
of longing.

As far as the opposite of
longing goes, I'm afraid
I don't know what to tell you.

As far as you go, I know
exactly what to tell you.

As far as you go
a honeysuckle choir.

As far as you go
a hatching of clouds.

As far as you go
my final migration,

as far as you go
my wing of a heart,

as far as you go

is as far as I go.

Bashert

I am coming.
In a beat-up Plymouth, powered by stars.
      Down a road of stars through trees of stars.
         Every button of my brand new suit is a star.
      My cufflinks, stars, I wear a star in my lapel.
I washed my hair with a handful of stars.
      The sky shaken loose, I lathered my beard.
         I am coming to you with a bouquet of stars.
      With a blanket of stars & a basket of stars.
With a bottle of stars & a banquet of stars.
      For years I have pulled stars from my body.
         Here is the joy, here is the grief, here is
    the slaughter I have shaped into stars.
I have polished the stars & buried them.
      An orchard has grown, it is heavy & yours.
         I will gather the fruit & transport it to you.
      See how it falls from my pockets & speaking.
My psalm is a star & the star is for you.
      My waltz is a star & the star is for you.
         We will hold these stars to each other's lips
    & drink the ghosts from each other's stars.
I am coming to you with a wedding of stars,
      a procession of stars, & a chuppah of stars,
         a book of stars with our song written in it.
      If the hush returns with its claws unbroken
we'll be here Sal, with stars in our knuckles,
      stars in our hammer, stars in our singing.
         A volley of stars will descend on our houses.
      A volley of stars will pummel this country.
The absence, eaten by packs of stars.

A voice will speak in the voice of a star.
      A voice will speak & the river will stand.
   The river will stand & I love you, Sally.
I love you, Sally & the river will carve
our names into the dark.

The Cantor Sings

here is the name of the country
       that picks your past from its teeth

here at the lip of the knife is the throat
       that used to sing you to sleep

here is the part of the story
       where a war hijacks your eyes

here is the part of the story
       where you must be the lullaby

Some Mischievous Angel
Has Looked Down & Saw Us

Amid the bombs. Amid the smoldering altars. Amid
the stars invisible for the smoke. Amid cudgeled jokes.
Amid children surrounded by walls of slaughtered
torahs. Amid bullet psalms & dollar psalms, the psalms
of abandonment. Amid soldiers turned chimney, spirits
twisting from the edge of tattered necks. Amid the czar's
blood ledgers. Amid brick-smashed synagogue windows.
Amid gunmetal trees & slogan-shaped flowers. Amid owls
interrogating each survivor quaking in the hours. Amid
the bruised syllables of the Kaddish. Amid the gibberish
of loss. Amid friends renamed for starlings & martyrs.
Amid the boats, the rot of the fruit. Amid all that non-
partisan water. Amid marriages to acts of subtraction.
Amid prayers flung like lilies through the arbitrary dark.
Amid the carved-out wings discarded in the fields on the
way from here to there. Amid the color-stripped air. Amid
a holocaust of auburn hair. Amid the rumbling hearts
of eggs. Amid red winters, red springs, red autumns, red
summers. Amid vaporized fathers & unraveled mothers.
Amid the pains that have been taken to turn our evens
odd, something blooms between two mouths—makes
sense, makes quiet, makes God.

Notes

The following titles/lines were taken from
Lanford Wilson's *Talley's Folly*:

"Whatever Time There Is in a Life Is a Lifetime"

"We will never be any use again…"

"I Will Tell This in the Only Way I Can Tell It"

"Eggs! Eggs! Eggs! Eggs!"

"But what good is an egg?"

"Amazing the Things You Get So Used to That You Don't Know Them Anymore"

"Some Mischievous Angel Has Looked Down & Saw Us"

*

Bashert—Yiddish word meaning "fated, destined," most commonly used to refer to one's "divinely ordained" soulmate.

Bobkes—Yiddish word meaning "cow dung, zero, nothing."

Boychik—Yiddish term of endearment for a young boy or young man.

Chuppah—the canopy under which Jewish couples stand during the wedding ceremony.

Gottenyu—Yiddish expression meaning "Oh God" or "Dear God."

Goyische—Hebrew/Yiddish term meaning "non-Jewish."

Gutte Neshome—Yiddish expression meaning "good soul."

HaShem—Hebrew word meaning "the Name," used in this context to refer to God.

Kaddish—a hymn of praise offered to God, used here specifically to refer to "the Mourner's Kaddish," a prayer spoken during mourning rituals in Judaism.

Kishka—various kinds of sausage/stuffed intestine originating in Eastern Europe and popular among Ashkenazi (central or eastern European) Jews.

Mishegas—Yiddish word meaning "craziness."

Pish—Yiddish word meaning "urine, urinate."

Rugalach—a crescent-shaped Jewish pastry.

Toches—Yiddish word meaning "buttocks."

Acknowledgements

Thanks to the editors of the following journals for giving a home to certain of the poems in this book:

Alien Mouth, Bodega, Drunk in a Midnight Choir, Epigraph, Fourth & Sycamore, The Harpoon Review, Leopardskin & Limes, Nailed, Potluck, Requited, Reservoir, Sundog Lit, Winter Tangerine.

Thanks to Art Cohan & Samantha Sloyan, without whom this book would & could not exist. Thank you for your constancy and kindness, your presence, your egg-breaking hearts. You are gutte neshomes & I love you both.

Thanks to Lanford Wilson for writing the play to which these poems owe their existence.

I am ever indebted to Daniel Lisi. For your unshaking support & belief, my dear friend, thank you.

Thank you to Hollis Hart, for never not dancing. What a mitzvah you are.

To Elaina Ellis, my attentive & extraordinary editor, I could not have made this without you. You lift me & you lift the word.

Thanks to Dalton Day & Shira Erlichman for looking at earlier versions of these poems/this book. Whatever is to be praised for your existence, I praise it.

I am grateful for the particular kindnesses of Genevieve Angelson, Clara Aranovich, Johnny Auer, Aziza Barnes, Allen Barton, Chelsea Bayouth, Edwin Bodney, Brandon Jordan Brown, Derrick Brown, Jessica Buttafuoco, Claire Cetera, Brendan Constantine, Christine Donlon, Brian S. Ellis, Bart Foley, Jorge Garcia, Alex & Fiona Gubelweed, April Henry, Roddy & Jessica Jessup, Sean & Randi Kearney, Aaron & Anastasia Leddick, Zarah Mahler, Mike McGee, Jessica Melia, Anis Mojgani, Amelia Morck, Angel Nafis, Mindy Nettifee,

Hieu Minh Nguyen, Emily O'Neill, Meghann Plunkett, April Ranger, Crystal Reed, Remy Remigio, Jon Sands, Mark & Ilana Saul, sam sax, Carter Scott, Lisa Schwartz, Danny Scuderi, Scott & Carla Sheldon, Alea Shurmantine, Kate Siegel, Christina Smith, Jayson Smith, Lauren Speer, Brynn Thayer, Nick Thurston, Alex Ustach, Buddy Wakefield, Alyesha Wise, Michael & Tania Gonzalez Yavnielli, Rebecca Zahler, & too many, too many others.

Enormous thanks to The Beverly Hills Playhouse, my home and synagogue for the last twelve years.

To my family, thank you. Bless you. L'Chaim.

To Kayla, my sister, my hero, thank God you're here.
None of this without you.

To my Grandma, Bess Radin,
you remain with us in every tenderness.

To my mother, all of my gratitude.
You have given me this world.

To my pops, everything, everything.
I miss you. I love you. I hear you.

To all who find themselves alone in a room & turning the pages of this book: I am with you.

About the Author

Jeremy Radin is a poet, actor, and teacher living in Los Angeles.

His poems have appeared in *Cosmonauts Avenue, Drunk in a Midnight Choir, Nailed, Reservoir, Sundog Lit, Union Station, Winter Tangerine, Wyvern*, and elsewhere. His first book, Slow Dance with Sasquatch, is available from Write Bloody Publishing. He teaches acting at The Beverly Hills Playhouse and is the current coach of the Get Lit Players. You may have seen him on *It's Always Sunny in Philadelphia* or crying into a pastrami sandwich at Wexler's Deli.

Follow him @germyradin

Printed in the USA
CPSIA information can be obtained
at www.ICGtesting.com
JSHW080006150824
68134JS00021B/2321

9 781945 649035